D0590158

First published in the UK by
New Internationalist Publications Ltd
55 Rectory Road
Oxford
OX4 1BW, UK

www.newint.org

The Little Book of Bright Spirits

Compilation © New Internationalist 2000

Printed on recycled paper by C&C Offset Printing Co. Ltd., Hong Kong.

Designed by Ian Nixon

British Library Cataloguing-in-Publication Data.

A catalogue record for this book is available from the British Library.

ISBN 1 869847 92 X

THE LITTLE
BOOK OF
BRIGHT
Spirits

Foreword

In this little book you have a world of spiritual wisdom in your hands, with timeless insights from around a hundred 'bright spirits' – some famous, others perhaps less so. Wherever and whenever they have lived, people have gained wisdom, spiritual insight and good common sense which can inspire us all.

From the heart of Europe to the heat and turmoil of pre-Independence India; from the prairies of America's Wild West to the courtyards of Lebanon; from the highlands of China to the rainforests of Brazil comes a range of inspirational thoughts which can liberate and motivate. Reflect, challenge, contemplate… and above all enjoy words from **Taslima Nasreen** to **Maya Angelou**; **Chief Seattle** to **Khalil Gibran**; from **Deepak Chopra** to **Chico Mendes** and many more.

Never give up

Once there was a great forest fire, and all the birds and animals rushed to escape. Humming Bird went to the river and collected a drop of water. The other birds laughed. 'What are you doing?' they asked. She replied, 'I'm doing what I can.'

Native American story.

False modesty

We ask ourselves, who am I to be brilliant, gorgeous, talented and fabulous? Actually, who are you not to be? You are a child of God. Your playing small doesn't help the world.

Nelson Mandela (1918-)
former President of South Africa,
in his inaugural address 1994.

You can't have one without the other

When you are joyous look deep into your heart and you shall find it is only that which has given you sorrow that is giving you joy.

When you are sorrowful, look again into your heart, and you shall see that in truth you are weeping for that which has been your delight.

Kahlil Gibran (1833-1931) Lebanese poet.

Learn to love

In love, you grow and come home to yourself. When you learn to love and to let yourself be loved, you come home to the hearth of your own spirit. You are warm and sheltered. This is the condition in which we grow.

John O'Donohue, contemporary Irish theologian and poet.

Cruel lessons

*P*roblems are the cutting edge that distinguishes between success and failure. Problems call forth our courage and our wisdom; indeed they create our courage and our wisdom. It is only because of problems that we grow mentally and spiritually.

M Scott Peck, contemporary US psychiatrist.

Enlightenment

He that hath light...
may sit in the centre
and enjoy bright day.

John Milton (1608-1674) British poet.

Real sin

Sin lies only in hurting other people unnecessarily. All other 'sins' are invented nonsense.

Robert A Heinlein (1907-1988)
US science fiction writer.

Reflections in the water

Human nature is like a pool of water. Cast a stone therein, it goes rough and broken; stir it, and it becomes foul; give it peace, let it rest, and it will reflect the face of heavens which lie over it.

Laurence Housman, contemporary playwright.

Points of reference

He was my North, my South, my East
and West,
My working week and my Sunday rest,
My noon, my midnight, my talk, my song;
I thought that love would last forever:
I was wrong.

WH Auden (1907-1973) British poet.

Making a discovery ·

When you make the finding yourself - even if you're the last person on Earth to see the light - you never forget it.

Carl Sagan (1934-1996) US astronomer.

Spend time wisely

To finish the moment, to find the journey's end in every step of the road, to live the greatest number of good hours, is wisdom.

Ralph Waldo Emerson (1803-1882) US poet.

Attention

People teach in the world
what I know to be true:
If you live violently
That is how you will die.

The *Tao Te Ching*, 13th century
classic text of Taoism.

A square peg

I was always on the side of the losers – the Spanish anarchists for example. I always felt completely out of tune with almost everything around me.

Noam Chomsky (1928-) US linguistic theorist and political activist.

Free thinker

Freedom is always and exclusively freedom for the one who thinks differently.

Rosa Luxemburg (1870-1919) Polish-born German revolutionary.

Weather forecast

Accept the weather as it comes and people as they are.

Haitian saying.

Balance and illumination

When you are mindful in times of rest, you are observant in times of movement. If you have self-mastery in times of rest, you can be decisive in times of movement. If you have stability in times of rest, actions will not lead to unfortunate results. Rest is the foundation of movement, movement is the potential of rest. When you do not lose the constant in movement and rest, your path will be illuminated.

The *Tao Te Ching*, 13th century classic text of Taoism.

Constructing your life

The area covered by your life is not as important as what you build on it.

African saying.

Inaction

How long shall they kill our prophets while we stand aside and look?

Bob Marley (1945-1981) Jamaican
composer and singer.

Beauty

Look! My *fatele**
That I am singing you now,
Explains the beauty of my village.
My Faipule and Pulenuku and my elders
I'll never forget you in my heart.
You are like a reflection in a mirror
With your beautiful way of life.

Ihaia Puka (b.1907) Tokelau song-poet.

*action song

Checks and balances

It's not people who aren't credit-worthy. It's banks that aren't people-worthy.

> **Muhammad Yunus**, contemporary Bangladeshi economist and founder of the Grameen Bank.

Feast and famine

We cannot have a feast on global resources while the world's poor struggle to survive on inhospitable lands. It is as simple as that. It is the rich who are making the world poorer. Environment and poverty are one crisis, not two.

> **Petra Kelly** (1947-1992) German Green politician.

Behavioural science

Everything has been figured out,
except how to live.

Jean-Paul Sartre (1905-1980)
French existentialist writer.

Ethics and the moral majority

Because people who are not religious have tended to extend their scepticism about religion to ethics as well, they have yielded the field of ethics to the religious right. This has allowed the right to pre-empt 'morality' for crusades against abortion and homosexuality.

Peter Singer (1946-) Australian philosopher and ethicist.

Big thinker

It's a wide world and there's a great deal in it, and one head is but a poor little room to study in after all.

John Ruskin (1819-1900) British artist and thinker.

Cerebral

We are what we think.
All that we are arises
With our thoughts.
With our thoughts,
We make our world.

Gautama Buddha (563-483 BC)
founder of Buddhism.

The quest

Without knowing who I am and why I am here, life is impossible.

Leo Tolstoy (1828-1920) Russian writer.

The summing up

In three words I can sum up everything I've learned about life: it goes on.

Robert Frost (1874-1963) US poet.

The tapestry of life

Some people weave burlap into the fabric of our lives, and some weave gold thread. Both contribute to make the whole picture beautiful and unique.

Anonymous.

Essential breath

If we live as we breathe, take in and let go, we cannot go wrong.

Clarissa Pinkola Estés, contemporary Mexican/US poet and healer.

At home with your roots

Know from whence you came. If
you know whence you came,
there are absolutely no limitations to
where you can go.

James Baldwin (1924-1987) US writer.

Measured advice

Speech is priceless
if you speak with knowledge.
Weigh it in the scales of the heart
before it comes from the mouth.

Kabir (1440-1518) Indian Sufi master.

Consequences

I don't want flowers at my funeral because
I know that they would be taken from
the forest.

Chico Mendes (1944-1988) Brazilian
rubber-tapper and environmentalist.

Never fear love

When love beckons to you, follow it,
Though its ways are hard and steep.
And when its wings enfold you, yield to it,
Though the sword hidden among its
pinions may wound you.
And when love speaks to you believe in it.
Though its voice may shatter your dreams
as the north wind lays waste the garden.

Kahlil Gibran (1833-1931) Lebanese poet.

Mother Nature

Protect and honor the earth, for the earth is like your mother.

Sufi wisdom.

Right response

Do what you should do when you should do it.
Refuse to do what you should not do;
And, when it is not clear, wait until you are sure.

Muhammad (c.570-632) founder of Islam.

Spineless

Some people develop a wishbone where their backbone should be.

Anonymous

Your greatest enemy

Your most hostile enemy is your soul, enclosed between your two sides.

Sufi saying.

Point of view

Because we do most things relying only on our own sagacity we become self-interested, turn our backs on reason, and things do not turn out well. As seen by other people this is sordid, weak, narrow and inefficient.

Yamamoto Tsunetomo (1658-1719)
Japanese philosopher.

Question of balance

My cancer helped me to be a little more laid-back, as they say, because I realised more sharply that there was literally not enough time to be nasty.

Archbishop Desmond Tutu (1931-   )
South African, Chair of the Truth
and Reconciliation Commission.

Children

Your children are not your children.
They are the sons and daughters
of Life's longing for itself.
They come through you but not from you,
And though they are with you yet they
belong not to you.
You are the bows from which your children
as living arrows are sent forth.

Kahlil Gibran (1833-1931) Lebanese poet

Relationships

The easiest kind of relationship is with ten thousand people, the hardest is with one.

Joan Baez (1941-)
US singer and civil rights activist.

True to oneself

The very least you can do in your life is to figure out what you hope for. And the most you can do is live inside that hope. Not admire it from a distance but live right in it, under its roof.

Barbara Kingsolver (1955-)
contemporary US writer.

High hope

My hopes are not always realized,
but I always hope.

Ovid (43BC-17AD) Roman poet.

Earthly body

The earth is part of our body, and we
never gave up the earth.

Toohoolhoolzote, Native American/
Wallowa prophet, 1877.

Farming rights

When the man [sic] who feeds the world by toiling in the fields is himself deprived of the basic rights of feeding, sheltering and caring for his own families, the whole community of man is sick.

Cesar Chavez (1927-1993) US labor leader

Life's rich

There is no wealth but life.

John Ruskin (1819-1900)
British artist and thinker.

A question of tolerance

Freedom of opinion can only exist when the government thinks itself secure.

Bertrand Russell (1872-1970) British philosopher.

One side of the story

The whites told only one side. Told it to please themselves. Told much that is not true. Only his own best deeds, only the worst deeds of the Indians, has the white man told.

Yellow Wolf of the Nez Percés, in 1879.

The big threat

I want to go back to Bangladesh, but it's dangerous. I can't lead a normal life. I can't walk alone in the street, not since 1990. I was attacked several times by fundamentalists and others who thought I was threatening to the patriarchal society.

Taslima Nasreen, contemporary Bangladeshi writer living in exile, in 1995.

A thousand images

For a thousand years people have killed one another in the name of God. The challenge of the next millennium? Can those who live differently live together? Can we recognise God's image in one who is not in our own image?

Jonathan Sachs, Chief Rabbi of the United Hebrew Congregation of the Commonwealth, in 1999.

Freedom

The only conception of freedom I can have is that of the prisoner or the individual in the midst of the State. The only one I know is freedom of thought and action.

Albert Camus (1913-1960) French writer.

The material world

You give but little when you give of your possessions.

It is when you give of yourself that you truly give.

For what are your possessions but things you keep and guard for fear you may need them tomorrow?

And what is fear of need but need itself?

Kahlil Gibran (1833-1931) Lebanese poet

Fragile freedom

Freedom is fragile and must be protected. To sacrifice it, even as a temporary measure, is to betray it.

Germaine Greer (1939-)
Australian feminist academic.

A question of choice

Freedom lies only in our innate human capacity to choose between different sorts of bondage, bondage to desire or self esteem, or bondage to the light that lightens all our lives.

Sri Madhava, Hindu guru.

Be positive

Work on having positive thoughts, pay particular attention to speaking positive words, then let the resultant positive feelings take care of everything else.

John O'Donohue, contemporary
Irish theologian and poet.

Priorities

An ethical approach to life does not forbid having fun or enjoying food and wine, but it changes our sense of priorities.

Peter Singer (1946-   ) Australian philosopher and ethicist.

Paying the bill

We gain freedom when we have paid the full price.

Rabindranath Tagore (1861-1941) Indian poet.

The stuff of dictatorship

True individual freedom cannot exist without economic security and independence. People who are hungry and out of a job are the stuff of which dictatorships are made.

Franklin D Roosevelt (1882-1945) US president.

Look to the other

We really have to understand the person we want to love. If our love is only a will to possess, it is not love. If we only think of ourselves, if we only know our own needs and ignore the needs of the other person, we cannot love. We must look deeply in order to see and understand the needs, aspirations and suffering of the person we love. This is the ground of real love.

Thich Nhat Hanh, Vietnamese Zen master.

Cheap

That which costs little is less valued.

Miguel de Cervantes (1547-1616)
Spanish novelist.

Question of perception

Riches get their value from the mind of the possessor; they are blessings to those who know how to use them, and curses to those who do not.

Terence (c.190–159BC) Roman playwright.

African dilemma

The biggest obstacle is that those who are in power are like one riding on the back of a tiger. And they really want almost a water-tight assurance before they get off because they feel if they get off the tiger's back, it will eat them.

Julius Nyerere (1922-1999) president of Tanzania, on the Rwanda/Burundi conflicts.

Your work

If you cannot work with love but only with distaste, it is better that you should leave your work.

Kahlil Gibran (1833-1971) Lebanese poet.

Kill-joy

People must not do things for fun. We are not here for fun. There is no reference to fun in any act of Parliament.

AP Herbert (1890-1971) UK politician.

Hedonism

Fun is a good thing but only when it spoils nothing better.

George Santayana (1863-1952)
Spanish-born US philosopher.

Which way?

The great thing in the world is not so much where we stand, as in what direction we are moving.

Oliver Wendell Holmes (1809-1894) US writer.

We've only just begun

A day is precious because each day is essentially the microcosm of your whole life. Each new day offers possibilities and promises that were never seen before. To engage with honour the full possibility of your life is to engage in a worthy way the possibility of your new day. Each day is different.

John O'Donohue, contemporary Irish theologian and poet.

Keep trying

Success is 99 per cent failure.

Soichiro Honda (1906-1991) Japanese founder
of Honda motor company.

Action

The world is in your hands, now use it.

Phil Collins, contemporary British musician.

Words and deeds

Knowing is not enough; we must apply.
Willing is not enough; we must do.

JW von Goethe (1749-1832) German poet.

Kindling the flames

The mind is not a vessel to be filled but
a fire to be kindled.

Plutarch (c.46-120 AD) Greek biographer
and philosopher.

Watch out

A person on tiptoe
Can't walk easily.

The one who strides on ahead is
bound to tire.

The kind of person who always insists
on his way of seeing things
can never learn anything from
anyone.

Those who always want to be seen
will never help others to be.

The *Tao Te Ching*, 13th century
classic text of Taoism.

To be or not

The world is getting to be such a dangerous place, a man is lucky to get out of it alive.

WC Fields (1879-1946) US actor.

Take it in your stride

All truly great thoughts are conceived by walking.

Friedrich Nietzsche (1844-1900)
German philosopher.

Fast learner

When I was a boy of fourteen, my father was so ignorant I could hardly stand to have the old man around. But when I got to be twenty-one, I was astonished at how much the old man had learned in seven years.

Josh Billings (1818-1885) US humorist.

Seeing beauty

Youth is happy because it has the ability to see beauty. Anyone who keeps the ability to see beauty never grows old.

Franz Kafka (1883-1924) Austrian writer.

Solace and the soul

The best remedy for those who are afraid, lonely or unhappy is to go outside, somewhere they can be quiet, alone with the heavens, nature and God. Because only then does one feel that all is as it should be and that God wishes to see people happy, amidst the simple beauty of nature. As long as this exists, and it certainly always will, I know that then there will always be comfort for every sorrow, whatever the circumstances may be. And I firmly believe that nature brings solace in all troubles.

Anne Frank (1929-1945) German-born Jewish diarist.

Wholeness

I have never thought of my life as divided between poetry and life.

Pablo Neruda (1904-1973) Chilean poet.

A closed mind

Too often the opportunity knocks, but by the time you push back the chain, push back the bolt, unhook the locks and shut off the burglar alarm, it's too late.

Rita Coolidge (1944-   ) US singer.

Opportunity

Enlarge the opportunity and the person will expand to fill it.

> **Eli Ginzberg** (b.1911) US health policy expert and writer.

Take the chance

When the doors of opportunity swing open, we must make sure that we are not too drunk or too indifferent to walk through.

> **Jesse Jackson** (1941-) US civil rights activist.

Equal opportunity

One can present people with opportunities. One cannot make them equal to them.

Rosamond Lehmann (1901-1990) British writer.

There's hope!

Even a blind dog can find a bone every so often.

Alexei Sayle, contemporary British comedian.

Keeping alert

Loss of freedom seldom happens overnight. Oppression doesn't stand on the doorstep with toothbrush moustache and swastika armband - it creeps up insidiously... step by step, and all of a sudden the unfortunate citizen realizes that it is gone.

Geoffrey Lane (1918-   ) British judge.

Ways of seeing

The original is unfaithful to the translation.

Jorge Luis Borges (1899-1986) Argentinian writer.

Having it all

You can have it all. You just can't have it all at one time.

Oprah Winfrey (1954-) US broadcaster.

Picture this

Imagine all the people living life in peace. You may say I'm a dreamer, but I'm not the only one. I hope someday you'll join us, and the world will be as one.

John Lennon (1940-1980) British musician.

Passionate possibility

If I were to wish for anything, I should not wish for wealth and power, but for the passionate sense of the potential, for the eye which, ever young and ardent, sees the possible. Pleasure disappoints, possibility never. And what wine is so sparkling, what so fragrant, what so intoxicating, as possibility!

Søren Kierkegaard (1813-1855)
Danish philosopher.

Means and ends

Peace is not merely a distant goal that we seek, but a means by which we arrive at that goal.

Martin Luther King (1928-1968)
US civil rights activist.

Peace of land

Peace is more precious than a piece of land.

Anwar Sadat (1918-1981) Egyptian president.

Thread of life

The Earth does not belong to Man, but He to the Earth. Man has not woven the web of life, he is only a thread in it. The air is something precious because all things share the same breath: animals, trees and man. If all the animals disappeared, man would die of a great loneliness of spirit.

Chief Seattle of the Suwamich nation, to the President of the United States in 1855.

Wildness

If you step out of the radius of your campfires you feel that you are brought face to face with forces over which you have no control; you are surrounded by handiwork that is not man's, by swarming millions of creatures that live out their little lives without the faintest reference to you.

Robert W C Shelford, contemporary naturalist.

Tuning in

The only tyrant I accept in this world is the still voice within.

MK Gandhi (1869-1948)
Indian nationalist leader.

Slowing down

The air is fragrant with summer-swamp scent – a blend of mud, algae, soapflower, and buttonbush. All around us is the sleepy music of summer swamp – the rattle of a kingfisher, the chucking of the now mostly quiet red-winged blackbirds, the banjo twang of green frogs, the buzz of cicadas starting in one red maple and picking up in another. I learned a long time ago that one of the things swamps are good for is slowing summers that go by too fast.

Ted Williams, contemporary US environmentalist.

Life's transition

How beautifully leaves grow old. How full of light and color are their last days.

John Burroughs (1837-1921)
US naturalist and author.

Stand fast

Be like a tree in pursuit of your cause: Stand firm, grip hard, thrust upward, bend to the winds of heaven, and learn tranquillity.

Edward Abbey, contemporary US writer

Beliefs

When you have people together who believe in something very strongly – whether it's religion or politics or unions – things happen.

Cesar Chavez (1927-1993) US labor leader.

A question of time and priorities

Ultimately love is everything. When we love something it is of value to us, and when something is of value to us we spend time with it, time enjoying it and time taking care of it.

M Scott Peck, contemporary US psychiatrist.

Scaling the heights

Never measure the height of a mountain, until you have reached the top. Then you will see how low it was.

Dag Hammarskjold (1905-1961) Swedish politician and UN secretary-general.

Wings to soar

The person who has no imagination has no wings.

Muhammed Ali/Cassius Clay (1942-) US boxer.

Telling all

There is no agony like bearing an untold story inside of you.

Maya Angelou (1928-) US poet.

Whitman's creed

This is what you shall: love earth and sun and animals, despise riches, give alms to anyone that asks, stand up for the stupid and crazy, devote your income and labor to others, hate tyrants, argue not concerning God.

Walt Whitman (1819-1889) US poet.

Play your part

The world is before you, and you need not take it or leave it as it was before you came in.

James Baldwin (1924-1987) US writer.

Ways of learning

If I am given a formula, and I am ignorant of its meaning, it cannot teach me anything. But if I already know it, what does the formula teach me?

St Augustine (354-430) early Christian.

World of wonder

The lasting pleasures of contact with the natural world are not reserved for scientists but are available to anyone who will place herself under the influence of earth, sea and sky, and their amazing life.

Rachel Carson (1907-1964)
US marine biologist and writer.

Our visage

Your face is the icon of your life. In the human face a life looks out at the world and looks in at itself. There is a strange symmetry in the way the soul writes the story of its life in the contours of the face.

John O'Donohue, contemporary Irish theologian and poet.

High notes

Music is the mediator between the spiritual and the sensual life.

Ludwig Van Beethoven (1770-1827)
German composer.

Being oneself

To be ourselves causes us to be exiled by many others, and yet to comply with what others want causes us to be exiled from ourselves.

Clarissa Pinkola Estés, contemporary
Mexican/US poet and healer

Here and now

Don't be afraid of death so much as an inadequate life.

Bertolt Brecht (1898-1956) German playwright.

An egomaniac

If being an egomaniac means I believe in what I do and in my art or my music, then in that respect you can call me that.... I believe in what I do, and I'll say it.

John Lennon (1940-1980) British musician.

Don't look back

If you must leave a place that you have lived in and loved and where all your yesterdays are buried deep - leave it any way except a slow way, leave it the fastest way you can. Never turn back and never believe that an hour you remember is a better hour because it is dead. Passed years seem safe ones, vanquished ones, while the future lives in a cloud, formidable from a distance. The cloud clears as you enter it. I have learned this but, like everyone, I learned it late.

Beryl Markham (1902-1986)
Kenyan/British aviator and writer.

The spark of genius

All the means of action - the shapeless masses, the materials - lie everywhere about us. What we need is the celestial fire to change the flint into the transparent crystal, bright and clear. That fire is genius.

Henry Longfellow (1807-1882) US poet.

Love and death

Love makes us poets and the approach of death makes us philosophers.

George Santayana (1863-1952)
Spanish-born US philosopher.

Conceit

Wind puffs up empty bladders, opinion, fools.

Socrates (469-399 BC) Greek philosopher.

Think about it

Enjoy life. There's plenty of time to be dead.

Anonymous.

Full life

May you live every day of your life.

Jonathan Swift (1667-1745)
Irish writer.

Progress?

With great difficulty advancing by millimetres each year, I carve a road out of the rock. For millennia my teeth have wasted and my nails broken to get there, to the other side, to the light and the open air. And now that my hands bleed and my teeth tremble, unsure in a cavity cracked by thirst and dust, I pause and contemplate my work. I have spent the second part of my life breaking the stones, drilling the walls, smashing the doors, removing the obstacles I placed between the light and myself in the first part of my life.

Octavio Paz, contemporary Mexican poet.

Daring

*W*e must dare to invent the future.

Thomas Sankara (1950-1987)
president of Burkina Faso.

Here and now

*D*o not dwell in the past, do not dream
of the future, concentrate the mind
on the present moment.

Gautama Buddha (563-483 BC) founder of Buddhism.

On constancy

Commitment is inherent in any genuinely loving relationship. Anyone who is truly concerned for the spiritual growth of another knows, consciously or instinctively that he or she can significantly foster that growth only through a relationship of constancy.

M Scott Peck, contemporary US psychiatrist.

Opposition

Great spirits have always encountered violent opposition from mediocre minds.

Albert Einstein (1879-1955)
German-born physicist.

Up to you

You must be the change you wish to see in the world.

MK Gandhi (1869-1948)
Indian nationalist leader.

Presents

I give you an emptiness,
I give you a plenitude,
Wherever you go
they'll go with you and
wherever you are you'll wonder,
smiling about the fullness
you can't add to and the emptiness
that you can fill.

Norman MacCaig, contemporary Scottish poet.

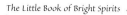

To inspire and aspire

Keep away from people who try to belittle your ambitions. Small people always do that, but the really great make you feel that you, too, can become great.

Mark Twain (1835-1910) US writer.

Lending a hand

Never look down on anybody unless you're helping them up.

Jesse Jackson (1941-) US civil rights activist.

At ease with yourself

When you are content to be simply yourself and don't compare or compete, everybody will respect you.

The *Tao Te Ching*, 13th century classic text of Taoism.

True happiness

The supreme happiness in life is the conviction that we are loved.

Victor Hugo (1802-1885) French writer.

Ignoring history

Those who do not remember the past are condemned to repeat it.

George Santayana (1863-1952)
Spanish-born US philosopher.

The classroom experience

There are no mistakes, no coincidences. All events are blessings given to us to learn from.

Dr Elisabeth Kubler-Ross (b.1927)
Swiss-born US psychiatrist and writer.

Go for it!

Nothing great was ever achieved without enthusiasm.

Ralph Waldo Emerson (1803-1882) US poet.

Opportunity

Every exit is an entry somewhere.

Tom Stoppard (1937-) British playwright.

After you

Teachers open the door, but you must enter by yourself.

Chinese Proverb.

Self-love

You, yourself, as much as anybody in the entire universe, deserve your love and affection.

Gautama Buddha (563-483 BC) founder of Buddhism.

Aim high

Shoot for the moon. Even if you miss, you'll land among the stars.

Les Brown (b.1912) US musician.

The linear system

Ecosystems sustain themselves in a dynamic balance based on cycles and fluctuations, which are non-linear processes. Linear enterprises, such as indefinite economic and technological growth - the storage of radioactive waste over enormous time spans - will necessarily interfere with the natural balance and, sooner or later, will cause severe damage.

Fritjof Capra, contemporary US physicist and writer.

Warts and all

A friend is one who knows you and loves you just the same.

Elbert Hubbard (1856-1915)
US publisher and author.

Dust to dust

People who fight fire with fire usually end up with ashes.

Abigail van Buren (b.1918) US journalist.

Body language

It is only with the heart that one can see rightly; what is essential is invisible to the eye.

Antoine de Saint-Exupéry (1900-1944)
French writer.

Love conquers

Darkness cannot drive out darkness; only light can do that. Hate cannot drive out hate; only love can do that.

Martin Luther King Jr (1928-1968)
US civil rights activist.

Big-heartedness

The less you open your heart to others, the more your heart suffers.

Deepak Chopra, contemporary
Indian-born doctor and writer.

Positive steps

Write the bad things that are done to you in sand, but write the good things that happen to you on a piece of marble.

Arab Proverb.

Soul food

A hug warms the soul and places a smile in the heart.

Anonymous.

Mandela's view

I have become more convinced than ever that the real makers of history are the ordinary men and women of our country; their participation in every decision about the future is the only guarantee of true democracy and freedom.

Nelson Mandela (1918-   )
South African anti-apartheid activist
and first black president, in 1990.

Imagination

Imagination is more important than knowledge. Knowledge is limited. Imagination encircles the world.

Albert Einstein (1879-1955) German-born physicist.

Transformation

After a time of decay comes the turning point. The powerful light that has been banished returns. There is movement, but it is not brought about by force... The movement is natural, arising spontaneously. For this reason the transformation of the old becomes easy. The old is discarded and the new is introduced. Both measures accord with time; therefore no harm results.

The *Tao Te Ching*, 13th century classic text of Taoism.

Hearing aid

Listen or thy tongue will keep thee deaf.

American Indian proverb.

Learning

Spoon-feeding in the long run teaches us nothing but the shape of the spoon.

EM Forster (1879-1970) British novelist.

Happiness

I have searched deep for its cause and found it. It does not lie in money or possessions or luxury; it does not lie in leisure or business, not in performance or consumption. In happy people I have always found the reason was deep security, spontaneous joy in small things and a great simplicity.

Phil Bosmans, contemporary Belgian priest.

Quest

To confine our attention to terrestrial matters would be to limit the human spirit.

Stephen Hawking (1942-) British physicist.

Ability

He is able who thinks he is able.

Gautama Buddha (563-483 BC)
founder of Buddhism.

Silver lining

If you want rainbows, you have to put up with the rain.

Dolly Parton (1946-) US singer.

Learning from experience

It was when I found out I could make mistakes that I knew I was on to something.

Ornette Coleman (1930-) US musician.

Don't stop

The world is so fast that there are days when the person who says it can't be done is interrupted by the person who is doing it.

Anonymous.

Sparklers

Diamonds are nothing more than chunks of coal that stuck to their jobs.

Malcolm Forbes (1919-   ) US publisher.

Daily tonic

The most wasted day of all is that during which we have not laughed.

Sébastian RN Chamfort (1740-1794)
French playwright.

Kindness

Deal gently with people and be not harsh; cheer them and do not condemn them.

Sufi saying.

Perception

To be able to see the right turns, we have to be able to see the wrong ones.

Clarissa Pinkola Estés, contemporary Mexican/US poet and healer.

Hidden depths

Each of us has much more hidden inside us than we have had a chance to explore. Unless we create an environment that enables us to discover the limits of our potential, we will never know what we have inside of us.

Muhammad Yunus, contemporary Bangladeshi economist and founder of the Grameen Bank.

Faith

The Lord is my light, and my salvation; whom shall I fear?

Psalm 27.

The future

The future belongs to those who believe in the beauty of their dreams.

Eleanor Roosevelt (1882-1945)
US diplomat and first lady.

Capacity

When I grow up
oh yes
when I grow up
I shall do many things.

Sam Ukala, contemporary
Nigerian writer.

Excellence

We are what we repeatedly do. Excellence, then, is not an act but a habit.

Aristotle (384-322 BC) Greek philosopher.

The future

As religious and spiritual people we base our lives on an Ultimate Reality and draw spiritual power and hope therefrom in trust, in prayer or meditation, in word or silence. We have a special responsibility for the welfare of all humanity and care for the planet Earth. We do not consider ourselves better than other women and men, but we trust that the ancient wisdom of our religions can point the way for the future.

Parliament of the World's Religions,
South Africa, in 1999.

Youth

Young people have exalted notions, because they have not been humbled by life or learned its necessary limitations. They overdo everything - they love too much, hate too much, and the same with everything else.

Aristotle (384-322 BC) Greek philosopher.

Experience

The most beautiful thing we can experience is the mysterious.

Albert Einstein (1879-1955)
German-born physicist.

Walk and talk

The true charm of pedestrianism does not lie in the walking, or in the scenery, but in the talking. The walking is good to time the movement of the tongue by, and to the blood and the brain stirred up and active; the scenery and the woodsy smells are good to bear in upon a man an unconscious and unobtrusive charm and to eye and soul and sense; but the supreme pleasure comes from the talk.

Mark Twain (1835-1910) US writer.

Angel's place

One should not stand at the foot of a sick person's bed, because that place is reserved for the guardian angel.

Jewish saying.

Now or never

Live as if you were to die tomorrow. Learn as if you were to live forever.

MK Gandhi (1869-1948) Indian nationalist leader.

Age

It is not all bad, this getting old, ripening. After the fruit has got its growth it should juice up and mellow. God forbid I should live long enough to ferment and rot and fall to the ground in a squash.

Emily Carr (1871-1945) Canadian artist.

An Aboriginal outlook

Active participation of Aboriginal people will renew Australian life during the 21st century. But it will need Aboriginal people who are strong and balanced, rooted in their families and their land. This will depend on Aboriginal people being educated as balanced contemporary Aboriginal Australians, something which will only happen when this education is inspired by their land.

Mandawuy Yunupingu, contemporary Aboriginal Australian educationist and musician.

Mind over matter

To restore the mind to its unfragmented origin, sit quietly and meditate: First count the breaths, then tune the breath until it is imperceptible; be mindful of the body as like the undifferentiated absolute, and you won't hear anything. Those who can regain their composure after a mountain crumbles before them are second best; not even being startled is expertise.

The *Tao Te Ching*, 13th century classic Taoist text.

About New Internationalist Publications

New Internationalist is a publications co-operative based in Oxford, UK, with editorial and sales offices in Aotearoa/New Zealand, Australia and Canada.

It publishes the **New Internationalist** magazine on global issues, which has 65,000 subscribers worldwide. The NI also produces the One World Calendar, Almanac and Greetings Cards, as well as publications such as *Eye to Eye: Women* and food books including *The Spices of Life* and *Vegetarian Quick & Easy* - cooking from around the world.

For more information write to:

Aotearoa/New Zealand PO Box 4499, Christchurch.
newint@chch.planet.org.nz

Australia and PNG 28 Austin Street, Adelaide 5000, South Australia.
helenp@newint.com.au

Canada and US 1011 Bloor Street West, Toronto, Ontario M6H 1M1.
reidmill@web.net

United Kingdom 55 Rectory Road, Oxford OX4 1BW. ni@newint.org

Visit the **NI** website at **www.newint.org**

THE LITTLE BOOK OF BIG IDEAS
Thoughts on the important things in life.

Collected by Vanessa Baird

'When an idea is wanting, a word can always be found to take its place,' said Goethe. This little book is the exact opposite. It's rich in ideas, economic in words. Put the world's greatest thinkers in your pocket. This little book captures the essence of some of the biggest ideas — from Gaia to Chaos theory, from Communism to Eco-Feminism, from the 'end of History' to racial equality. It provides food for both cogitation and inspiration — ideal for the busy person with more brain than time. In their own words, enjoy the ideas and ideals of thinkers and activists such as:

James Lovelock, Vandana Shiva, EF Schumacher, Eduardo Galeano, Angela Davis, Francis Fukuyama, James Gleick, Nelson Mandela, Audre Lorde, Socrates, Kenneth Kaunda, Karl Marx, Bertrand Russell, Mahatma Gandhi, Albert Einstein, Germaine Greer, Mark Twain, the Dalai Lama.

This small book will easily fit into a handbag or pocket. It can be read right through or dipped into and used on a 'thought for the day' basis, on the bus, on the train, anywhere.

ISBN 1 869847 79 2

THE LITTLE BOOK OF GREAT WOMEN

Thoughts from women who changed the world

Forget 'Little Women'. Forget demure damsels, neatly tucked
into the mental corsets of patriarchy. This is the book of women
who challenged and changed the world. The Great Women we
mean range from Hypatia to Goldman; de Beauvoir to Roy;
Allende to el Saadawi. Enjoy the thoughts, deeds and exploits of
women who have made their mark and those who continue to
do so.

A truly international little book, including a good selection of
often under-represented African, Latin American, Asian and
African-American women of note.

◆ User-friendly
◆ Small in size but large enough in subject matter to fully engage
the grey cells.
◆ Ideal for the busy person with more brain than time.

ISBN 1 869847 91 1
See all our products on the NI website at
www.newint.org